INDEPENDENCE DAY AT HAPPY MEADOWS

by
Laura King

STEELE SPRING
STAGE RIGHTS
www.stagerights.com

INDEPENDENCE DAY AT HAPPY MEADOWS
Copyright © 2016 by Laura King
All Rights Reserved

For all stage performance inquiries, please contact:

Steele Spring Stage Rights
3845 Cazador Street
Los Angeles, CA 90065
(323) 739-0413
www.stagerights.com

INDEPENDENCE DAY AT HAPPY MEADOWS

CAST OF CHARACTERS

5F, 1M

SHIRLEY: Excitable, nervous, older woman

BETTY: Sarcastic, no-nonsense, older woman

MARY: Sweet, Southern, older woman

HOLLY: Determined, intelligent, older woman

NANCY: Self-serving, controlling, middle-aged woman

GUS: Gruff, blue-collar, middle-aged man

SCRIPT NOTES

In Nancy's telephone monologue, directors have permission to change the reference to Luray Caverns to another inexpensive vacation spot better known to their audience.

SETTINGS

The common room and administration office of Happy Meadows Nursing Home; Holly's farmhouse

INDEPENDENCE DAY AT HAPPY MEADOWS

ACKNOWLEDGMENTS

Special thanks to everyone who has supported this play during its development, particularly James Beck, Todd Ristau, Robert Moss, and Judith Beasley. Thanks to my father Richard King, my sister Lynn Hazlewood, and especially my mother, Ressie King, and her sisters, Dottie Nicely, Lauranna Robertson, and Kathy Elick, who inspired this play. And, as always, love and deep gratitude to Mark and Katie King.

ACT I

SCENE 1

THE COMMON ROOM AT HAPPY MEADOWS NURSING HOME

MARY and BETTY are seated at a table with plates of food in front of them. SHIRLEY is in a wheelchair, wheeling back and forth in a pacing motion. HOLLY is on the couch reading a letter.

SHIRLEY: I can't take it anymore, I tell you. I can't take it.

SHIRLEY twitches.

BETTY *(looking disgustedly at her food and dropping her fork)*: Here we go again.

MARY: Calm down, Shirley.

SHIRLEY: I can't calm down, Mary. I'm going stir-crazy.

BETTY: Or just plain crazy.

SHIRLEY: What did you say?

BETTY: Nothing.

MARY: Everything will be all right, sugar.

BETTY: Keep telling her that, Little Mary Sunshine.

MARY: I told you to stop calling me that.

BETTY: If you ever take off those rose-colored glasses you're always wearing, I'll give you a new nickname.

MARY: Or you can just call me Mary. Just plain Mary.

BETTY: Okay, Just Plain Mary. That's what I'll call you.

MARY: That's not what I meant and you know it.

SHIRLEY: You two are making me a nervous wreck.

SHIRLEY twitches.

HOLLY: Would you all please shut up.

MARY, BETTY, and SHIRLEY are instantly quiet.

MARY: We're sorry.

SHIRLEY: Is everything all right, Holly?

HOLLY: I just need a little peace and quiet for once.

BETTY: We'll leave you alone then.

MARY *(whispering)*: She doesn't need to be left alone. Something's obviously bothering her.

BETTY *(whispering)*: I don't know what's wrong, but she hasn't been herself for weeks.

MARY: I know. Last week when Mr. Munsen changed the channel during "The Bridge on the River Kwai," she didn't even bat an eye.

BETTY: The old Holly would have tied him to his motorized scooter and put it in reverse.

MARY: Maybe she needs someone to talk to.

SHIRLEY wheels up to HOLLY.

SHIRLEY: Do you need someone to talk to, Holly?

HOLLY: No, I'm fine.

HOLLY crumples up the letter and throws it in a trash can, crosses to the table, and starts to push the food around on her plate. SHIRLEY follows Holly, BETTY sits on the couch, and MARY retrieves the letter from the trash can and starts to read it.

SHIRLEY: Are you sure? Having someone to talk to makes things a lot more bearable in here.

HOLLY: Look, Shirley, I know you mean well, but I really just want to be left alone.

SHIRLEY: I'll just sit here and keep you company then.

HOLLY: Suit yourself.

MARY crosses to BETTY to show her the letter.

MARY *(whispering)*: Betty, look at this.

BETTY *(whispering)*: What are you doing with that?

MARY *(whispering)*: I had to find out what was wrong with her. It's from her grandson.

BETTY *(whispering)*: I don't have my glasses. Read it to me.

MARY *(whispering)*: Dear Grandma, Dad told me that you can't come home for the Fourth of July, but I don't know why. You've always been here before. And this is a really important one. The last one in our house. Dad told me he had to sell it to pay for your new place. I don't know where we're going, but we're not going to be here anymore. Please try to come home. Even if it's just for the day. Love, Jimmy.

BETTY *(whispering)*: Oh, man, no wonder she's so moody.

MARY *(whispering)*: Poor old thing.

BETTY *(whispering)*: You better put that back in the trash before she sees you.

MARY crosses back to the trashcan.

SHIRLEY: What you got there, Mary?

MARY freezes and HOLLY looks up.

HOLLY: Is that my letter?

HOLLY crosses to MARY.

MARY: I'm sorry.

HOLLY snatches the letter away from MARY.

HOLLY: You've always been a snoop, Mary.

MARY: I wasn't snooping. I just wanted to know what was bothering you.

HOLLY: Well, now you do. Now everybody does.

SHIRLEY: I don't.

HOLLY: Then, by all means, let's bring you up to speed. This is a letter from Jimmy asking me to come home for the Fourth of July.

SHIRLEY: That's nice.

HOLLY: No, it's not nice, Shirley. I've told you all about him. You know he's only 10. He doesn't understand that I'm locked up here and can't get back to him.

MARY: Doesn't he know about your heart condition?

HOLLY: I never told him. I didn't want to scare him.

MARY: Can't Jimmy come here for the Fourth of July?

HOLLY: I don't want him to come here. I want him to remember me the way I was on the farm.

MARY: How was that?

HOLLY: Happy and strong. In my prime, I could do the work of any man. But those days are gone now. I'm nothing but a burden to them.

MARY: I'm sure your family doesn't feel that way.

HOLLY: Well, I do. Plus, Jack only kept the farm going for me. He knew I loved it. Now that I'm out of the way, he's free to move away. That's what he really wants.

MARY: But what about Jimmy?

HOLLY: Jimmy will be with his father. That's where he should be. It'll be hard on him to leave the farm, though. He loves it as much as I do.

BETTY: It's hard to leave your home.

MARY: But you didn't have a home, Betty. You were an army brat.

BETTY: We moved around a lot, but we were stationed at Fort Eustis the longest. That was my home.

MARY: What was so special about it?

BETTY: My dad was in the Transportation Corps there during World War II. That's where he taught me all about cars. He said I was a natural.

MARY: Is that what you did when you went in the army?

BETTY: That's what I wanted to do, but the army in all its infinite wisdom decided my skills would be better suited to typing and stenography.

HOLLY: That's probably what gave you the ulcers.

BETTY: Probably. But at least I'm close to Fort Eustis again.

MARY: Your home.

SHIRLEY: Everybody needs a home. No matter what age they are.

MARY: I had a great home.

SHIRLEY: Macon, Georgia.

MARY: That's right.

BETTY: Not like we could ever forget.

MARY: I know I talk about it a lot, but it gets me through.

HOLLY: Through what?

MARY: The loneliness.

SHIRLEY: Are you lonely, Mary?

MARY: Sometimes at night. That's when the memories come.

BETTY: Are they bad memories?

MARY: Oh, no. They're wonderful memories.

SHIRLEY: Like what?

MARY: Like when I was young and growing up in Macon. When I still had my Mama and Daddy and my brother Bobby.

SHIRLEY: That sounds nice.

MARY: Those were the best days of my life. It about killed me when I had to leave that place.

BETTY: You don't have to be here.

MARY: I didn't know where else to go. Everyone was gone. I'd never in my whole life been alone before. I wasn't sure I could take care of myself, so I came to Happy Meadows. It's okay here, but Macon will always be home.

SHIRLEY: What made Macon so special?

MARY: The little things. Riding my pony, wading in the creek, swinging on my tire swing. My daddy used to tell me he was going to cut that tire loose one day while I was swinging and it would roll me straight into Old Man Dickerson's pond.

BETTY: You had a pond?

MARY: We had a creek, but Old Man Dickerson on the next farm over had a great fishing pond.

BETTY: Did he let you fish in it?

MARY: No, he didn't let us, but we fished in it anyway. Old Man Dickerson was the meanest man in town. I was terrified of him but not Bobby. Bobby said that since that lake wasn't man-made, it didn't belong to Mr. Dickerson; it only belonged to God. And God loves children, and since we were children God would want us fishing in his lake. So every Sunday morning in the summer, Bobby and I would sneak over to that lake and try to catch some fish for breakfast.

BETTY: Did you ever catch any?

MARY: Oh, sure. Then we'd take them back to Mama, who would fry them up for us. She always pretended she didn't know where we got them. She said they were pretty big fish to come out of our little creek, but I think she liked that we put one over on that crabby Mr. Dickerson.

BETTY: I think I would have liked going fishing every Sunday.

MARY: Maybe you'll get a chance someday.

BETTY: There you go with those rose-colored glasses again.

MARY: There's nothing wrong with having a little optimism.

BETTY: Except when it borders on the delusional.

MARY: That's just like you. We were finally talking instead of bickering and you have to go and ruin it. Why do you have to be so antagonistic?

BETTY: Spare me your five dollar words. We all know you went to finishing school. And don't get any crazy ideas about us connecting.

MARY: Of course, not, because you'd just rather go on being a lonely sad-sack wallowing in her own misery.

BETTY: It's better than being a past-her-prime Southern matron who still considers herself the belle of the ball. Get a clue, sweetheart, the clock has struck midnight and the jig is up.

SHIRLEY: Enough! Can't you two stop fighting long enough to see that Holly needs us?

MARY: I'm sorry, Holly.

BETTY: Yeah, me too. What can we do?

HOLLY: There's nothing anybody can do. If I could only get home one more time, Jimmy and I could say goodbye together, and we'd have a last memory to hang on to.

SHIRLEY: Why can't you?

HOLLY: What?

SHIRLEY: Why can't you leave?

BETTY: Because the screws would be down on her so fast that her head would spin.

MARY: Shirley, you know they won't let us leave.

SHIRLEY: I'm not talking about asking for permission.

HOLLY: You mean a breakout?

SHIRLEY: Why not?

HOLLY: It would just be for one day. And it's July Fourth.

BETTY: This place is going to be a madhouse.

HOLLY: Nobody would even notice if I was gone. I could sneak out, go see Jimmy, say goodbye to the house, and be back before bed check.

SHIRLEY: We.

HOLLY: What?

SHIRLEY: We could sneak out and be back before bed check.

HOLLY: You want to go with me?

SHIRLEY: I need to go with you. I've been in here longer than any of you. Eight and a half years. Ever since the doctor said I needed supervision.

MARY: Because of the...

MARY taps her head with her finger.

SHIRLEY: I'm not crazy!

MARY: Nobody said you were crazy, sugar.

SHIRLEY: Take me with you, Holly. I need a change of scenery. I'm starting to get kind of squirrelly.

BETTY: Starting to?

SHIRLEY: Squirrelly Shirley, that's what everyone's going to call me if I don't get a break from this place. Squirrelly Shirley.

MARY: It's okay, honey.

SHIRLEY: Seriously, if I don't get out of here I might run amok.

BETTY: At least that would be something new. I'm so sick of staring at these same four walls I could scream. I need a little adventure, so count me in. What about you, Sunshine?

MARY: Me?

BETTY: You up for a road trip?

MARY: I'm not sure this is a good idea.

BETTY: Come on. It's the Fourth of July.

SHIRLEY: Don't we all deserve a little freedom?

MARY: Well, I wouldn't want to be left out.

SHIRLEY: That's the spirit.

MARY: One for all and all for one, I guess.

BETTY: What do you say, Holly?

HOLLY circles the women, critically inspecting them.

HOLLY: It might be good to have some allies. This kind of mission is notoriously dangerous. Did you ever see The Dirty Dozen?

MARY: Didn't they all die?

HOLLY: That's beside the point.

BETTY: So, we can come?

HOLLY: On one condition.

SHIRLEY: What's that?

HOLLY: You all have to pull your own weight. I'm not going to have time to deal with any screw-ups. This is my one chance to get home to Jimmy.

SHIRLEY: We won't screw-up, Holly. We promise.

HOLLY: Are we all agreed?

> HOLLY extends her hand. The other WOMEN pile their hands on top of Holly's hand.

BETTY, SHIRLEY & MARY: Agreed.

HOLLY: Today we bust out of Happy Meadows Nursing Home.

> The women throw their hands in the air and cheer.

SCENE 2

An office with a closet and a window. NANCY is seated at the desk. The telephone rings. Nancy answers the phone.

NANCY *(speaking into the phone)*: Happy Meadows Nursing Home. How can we make your day happier? Yes, this is Nancy. Who is this? Who? Oh, hello, Inspector Monroe. How can I help you? You're what? Today? But I don't understand. Why today? It's the Fourth of July. I see. No, it's no problem. Yes, that's fine. Is there a number where I can reach you? *(Writing down a phone number)* Got it. Thanks for the warning. I mean, for letting me know. Goodbye. *(Hanging up the phone and dialing a new number)* Why isn't anything ever easy around here? *(Speaking into the phone)* Gus? It's Nancy. Where are you? Well, haul your butt back to the warehouse. We've got a change in plans. I need the good stuff. I just got a call from the state inspector and he's coming by today. I don't know why. Maybe it's just routine or maybe he's getting complaints. I try to do my best for these old coots, but they don't appreciate me. If they can find a way to stir up trouble, they do. Look, Gus, I don't want to hear it. You wouldn't last a minute in this job. You're too big a softy. I do what I've got to do to make sure this place keeps running and turns a profit. My job is on the line. And you know what happens if I lose my job, don't you? No money for Nancy, no good life for Gus. No more fancy dinners, no more vacations to Luray Caverns, and no more me. You'll go back to being a lonely schlub who delivers cut-rate meat to old folks. Is that what you want? I didn't think so. Now here's the plan. It's July Fourth, so we're going to have a picnic. We're going to serve top-of-the-line food. That ought to make the residents happy, and happy residents means a happy inspector. After we get through today, we'll go back to business as usual. No excuses, Gus. I don't care if you're low on gas and oil, just get that tin truck of yours in gear. I'll meet you in the kitchen. Now move it.

NANCY hangs up the telephone and presses an intercom that transmits to the entire nursing home.

Attention, residents. Happy Fourth of July to one and all. Today is a very special day at Happy Meadows. In celebration of our country's independence, we will be having a picnic. I invite all residents and employees to meet by the front door at noon so we can head down to the lake to share this holiday together. Remember, it's a special day, so everyone should be on their best behavior. That means put on your brightest smiles and leave your problems at the door.

NANCY turns off the intercom.

And, for the love of all things holy, no stirring up any trouble.

SCENE 3

The common room.

HOLLY *(jumping up)*: Perfect!

MARY: What?

HOLLY: Didn't you hear what she said?

BETTY: She said it was the Fourth of July. Big news flash.

SHIRLEY: Even I knew that.

HOLLY: The other part. About meeting outside for the picnic.

BETTY *(alluding to the food)*: If this is the slop they're serving at the picnic, you can count me out.

MARY: You can send my regrets as well.

HOLLY: We'll all be sending our regrets. We have other plans.

SHIRLEY: What plans?

HOLLY: The breakout!

BETTY: Stay with us, Shirley.

HOLLY: Don't you all see? With everyone at the picnic, it's the perfect time for us to make our escape.

MARY: I don't know, Holly.

BETTY: Don't get cold feet now, Chicken Little.

MARY: But how are we going to manage it?

HOLLY: We need to get organized. Betty, grab that evacuation map off the wall. We need to locate our easiest exit.

> *BETTY grabs a laminated map off the wall, causing several chunks of plaster to fall to the floor. She hands the map to HOLLY. EVERYONE gathers around Holly.*

We can't go out the front door. That's where everyone will be meeting for the picnic. The back door leads to the fenced-in area. That's locked up tight as a drum. That leaves the kitchen.

MARY: But Holly, residents aren't allowed in the kitchen. If someone saw the four of us waltz in there together, they would know we were up to something.

HOLLY: No one's going to see us. Everyone's going to be at the picnic.

MARY: But what if somebody needs something in the kitchen? You can't guarantee that we won't get caught.

HOLLY: Look, girls. I don't have any guarantees for you, but if we pool our resources, I know we'll get out of here.

SHIRLEY: I'm not sure I have any resources.

MARY: Of course, you do, honey.

HOLLY: We all do. The more I think about it, the more I'm sure we have the makings of a crack breakout team.

BETTY: Us?

HOLLY: Remember the movie they showed us last week?

MARY: Stalag 17?

HOLLY: No, The Great Escape.

BETTY: I love The Great Escape.

MARY: James Garner was perfection.

SHIRLEY: I loved Steve McQueen. You never knew what he was going to do no matter how many times you saw it.

BETTY: You two would be a match made in heaven.

SHIRLEY: Oooh, let's watch it again.

HOLLY: We're not going to watch it. We're going to live it.

BETTY: We're going to lead World War II POWs out of a German prison camp?

HOLLY: No, we're going to lead four old ladies out of a dilapidated nursing home, and James Garner and Steven McQueen are going to help us.

MARY: How?

HOLLY: Remember in the movie when they were planning the breakout? They needed four main people— a mastermind, a scrounger, a lookout, and a decoy.

SHIRLEY: Oooh, I want to be the mastermind. Can I be the mastermind, Holly?

BETTY: Oh, Lord, help us. You're one part shy for that job, Shirley.

MARY: Hush, Betty, don't upset her. She's just forgetful.

BETTY: It's not that she's forgetful, it's that she's crazy.

SHIRLEY: Crazy? Did you call me crazy?

MARY: Settle down, Shirley. Betty didn't mean anything by it.

SHIRLEY: You know I don't like to be called crazy.

MARY: Nobody thinks you're crazy. You're just a little...

BETTY: Deranged?

MARY: Eccentric.

SHIRLEY *(pouting):* I just wanted to help Holly with the masterminding.

HOLLY: I think I can handle the mastermind role, Shirley. The first job we need to fill is the scrounger.

MARY: That doesn't sound very pleasant. What's a scrounger?

HOLLY: Someone in charge of supplies. It's not that far, but I want to be prepared in case we run into trouble.

SHIRLEY: Oooh, can I be the scrounger, Holly? I like the sound of that—scrouuunger.

HOLLY: Actually, I figured Mary would be a natural for the job. Are you up for it?

MARY: I'm flattered, Holly, but I don't know if I'm qualified. What do I have to do?

HOLLY: We'll need some food.

MARY: I'm really not much of a cook. Back when I was a girl in Macon, Georgia, Marvel Ann, our cook, always prepared our meals.

BETTY: We're not asking you to cook the food, just procure it.

MARY (reaching into her purse for a pencil and notebook): Oh, I see. Let me make a grocery list.

BETTY: You don't have time to get to the A&P, Mary.

HOLLY: You can take whatever we need from the kitchen.

MARY: I don't feel right about stealing food, Holly.

BETTY: Then you have nothing to worry about since what they serve here is definitely not food.

HOLLY: Just take what we would have eaten if we were staying for the picnic today.

MARY: I guess that's okay. What else do I have to do?

HOLLY: We'll need some comfortable clothes.

SHIRLEY: Yeah, we've got to be able to move with cat-like agility.

BETTY: Good luck with that.

MARY: I do have an eye for color, although I'm not sure what one wears to break out of a nursing home. I'll give it my best shot.

HOLLY: Good girl. Next we need a lookout. There's no guarantee that somebody won't wander away from the picnic and back into the kitchen.

BETTY: We need eyes on the ground.

HOLLY: Exactly.

BETTY: I'm on it.

HOLLY: Good, girl, Betty. You're just who I had in mind.

BETTY: What's the plan?

HOLLY: You've got to watch the kitchen and give us the all-clear signal when no one is within range.

BETTY: What kind of signal do you want?

HOLLY: I'll leave that to you. Just make sure we can hear it.

BETTY (lets loose with an earsplitting whistle): How's that?

HOLLY: That ought to do it.

BETTY: All right, count on me. I'll stand sentry duty.

MARY: But Holly, I still think it's too risky. It's a picnic after all. The staff will have to get into the kitchen to replenish the food.

BETTY: Who'd want to replenish that food?

SHIRLEY: And don't forget Creepy Larry.

MARY: That's right. He's supposed to sweep up but all he does is stand around smoking and dropping ashes on the floor.

BETTY: And his favorite place to smoke is the kitchen.

SHIRLEY: I don't like that Creepy Larry. He's...

BETTY: Creepy?

SHIRLEY: Yeah, creepy.

MARY: How are we going to make sure Larry or anyone else on staff doesn't see us?

HOLLY: That's where Shirley comes into play.

SHIRLEY: Me? What do you want me to do, Holly? Overpower Larry, take his broom, and subdue him? I can do it!

MARY: I really don't think we should be overpowering the janitors. It doesn't seem right. They're just providing a service.

BETTY: Plus, we might be getting a touch long in the tooth to do much overpowering.

HOLLY: We're not going to be doing any overpowering.

SHIRLEY: Darn. How about disguises? Are we going to need disguises?

MARY: Oh, that sounds good. I love to dress up. I have a lovely red hat with a peacock feather from my club days.

BETTY (sarcastically): Yeah, nobody would notice an old broad with a red peacock hat.

MARY: You don't have to be so dismissive. I have other hats as well.

BETTY: Oh, for Pete's sake. Would you forget the hats? Our biggest problem isn't going to be your head; it's going to be your mouth.

MARY (reaching for her mouth): What's wrong with my mouth?

BETTY: It's too big. You talk nonstop to everyone who comes in this place.

MARY: I'm a conversationalist. All Southern ladies understand the fine art of conversation.

BETTY: Oh, you're ladylike all right. You stage a full-frontal assault on every visitor that comes through the front door. Last week you dragged that man from room to room looking for his family.

MARY: A good hostess sees to the needs of all her guests.

BETTY: That's fine, Martha Stewart, but he was the mailman.

MARY: Well, he looked like he needed help.

BETTY: You're the one who needs help. It's like you have a social disease.

MARY: I beg your pardon.

BETTY: You've been oversocialized. You're still playing the part of the debutante. I swear I would die happy if I could go the rest of my life without hearing you start a sentence with the phrase, "Back when I was a girl in Macon, Georgia."

MARY: Just because I was raised right...

BETTY: Here we go.

MARY: Listen, Betty, back when I was a girl in Macon...

> *Realizing what she has just said, MARY covers her mouth.*

HOLLY: All right, are we done here?

BETTY: Sorry, Sarge, go ahead.

HOLLY: Thank you. Now, as I was saying, we're going to need a decoy to scare off the delivery man and anyone who wanders away from the picnic. We've got to get everyone away from the kitchen.

SHIRLEY: Is that me, Holly? Do I get to be the decoy? Oh, if I don't get to be the decoy, I don't know what I'll do.

HOLLY: Are you sure you're up for it, Shirley?

SHIRLEY: Of course, I'm up for it. Don't let the wheelchair fool you. Please give me a chance.

HOLLY: You'll have to create some kind of diversion.

SHIRLEY: I can do that. Maybe I could set off the fire alarm.

HOLLY: We don't want to alert the outside authorities.

SHIRLEY: I could ride naked in my wheelchair through the hallways.

MARY: That might be a bit extreme, dear. And we don't want you to catch a cold.

SHIRLEY: I could announce at the picnic that we're out of sweet tea.

BETTY: Don't do that. You might start a riot.

SHIRLEY: Don't worry, girls. I'll think of something.

HOLLY: All right then, Shirley. You're our decoy. Now, remember, at exactly noon you have to make sure everyone stays out of the kitchen.

SHIRLEY: I can do it. You can count on me.

BETTY: What about you, Holly? What are you going to be doing?

HOLLY: I'm going to make sure nobody interferes with our plans.

SHIRLEY *(whispering):* Are you talking about you know who?

HOLLY: That's right.

MARY: Nurse Nancy?

BETTY: Nurse Nasty is more like it.

HOLLY: Nancy or Nasty, she's no nurse.

BETTY: But heaven help anybody who doesn't call her that.

MARY: I think she wants us to acknowledge her authority.

BETTY: I think she wants us to prop up her delusions of grandeur.

SHIRLEY: I think she's the one who's crazy.

HOLLY: Whatever the case, I'm going to make sure that woman is as far away from the kitchen as possible.

MARY: I'm glad that's your job.

BETTY: I can't stand to be anywhere near that woman.

SHIRLEY: I don't like the way she smells.

MARY: How does she smell?

SHIRLEY: Like Pine-Sol and power.

SHIRLEY shudders.

MARY: Be careful, Holly.

HOLLY: Don't worry. I can handle her.

NANCY enters. SHIRLEY nudges HOLLY.

NANCY: Am I interrupting something, ladies?

Silence.

What are you all doing in here? It's almost time for the picnic.

Silence.

You four need to clear out of here. I'm expecting a delivery any minute.

Silence.

Look, I don't know what you're up to, but this picnic needs to go well, so no shenanigans today.

HOLLY: What do you mean?

NANCY: You know perfectly well what I mean.

HOLLY: I don't recall being a part of any shenanigans, Nancy.

NANCY: That's Nurse Nancy.

HOLLY: Sorry. Nurse Nancy.

NANCY: Think hard, Holly. I'm sure it will come to you.

HOLLY: I have no idea what you are referring to.

NANCY: How about the time you greased the wheels of Mr. Armstrong's wheelchair with butter and slid him into the cafeteria at dinner time?

HOLLY: Oh, that.

NANCY: Yes, that.

HOLLY: He was tired of always being the last served. For some reason, that man loves the cuisine here. He can't get enough of the stewed prunes and tomato bisque.

NANCY: Or what about the time in arts and crafts when you decided to cross-stitch inappropriate sayings in your sampler?

HOLLY: "Roses are red, violets are blue, this place sucks, and so do you." It's not Emily Dickinson, but I thought it had a certain emotional truth to it.

NANCY: And the time you hacked into our cable service and got Skinemax for free?

HOLLY: That was a movie night we'll never forget.

NANCY: You almost gave Mr. Daniels a heart attack.

HOLLY: At least he would have gone out with a smile on his face.

NANCY: So, you'll forgive me for being suspicious.

HOLLY: Yes, you're forgiven... for that.

NANCY: Thank you. Now clear up those breakfast dishes. This place needs to be spic-and-span today. I'll be back in a bit to make sure everything is in order.

NANCY exits.

HOLLY: Did you hear what she said?

MARY: She's expecting a delivery.

BETTY: I bet it's more of that repulsive creamed corn.

MARY: Is it creamed corn, Holly?

BETTY: If it is I don't want anything to do with it.

HOLLY: How should I know? And I'm not asking you to eat it.

BETTY: Good because there's no way I'm eating that stuff.

HOLLY: Can you please shut up and listen to me?

BETTY: Sorry.

HOLLY: It's the last piece of the puzzle.

MARY: What do you mean?

HOLLY: We've accounted for surveillance, supplies, and the escape route, but we were missing one vital ingredient, and it was just dropped in our laps.

BETTY: What?

HOLLY: The getaway vehicle!

MARY: Holly, you don't mean we're going to steal the delivery man's truck?

HOLLY: Of course, not. Look, it's simple. Betty will signal us when the delivery man finishes unloading the truck. Then Shirley will cause a disturbance, distracting the delivery man as well as any other staff. When everyone runs to see the cause of the commotion, we'll all simply slip out when no one is looking and hide in the truck. When the delivery man returns, he'll drive us right past Nurse Nasty and off the grounds.

MARY: Then what?

BETTY: How do we get back to your place?

SHIRLEY: Maybe we could ask the delivery man to drop us off at Holly's farm.

BETTY: More than likely he'd drop us off at the nut farm.

MARY: Where exactly is your place, Holly?

HOLLY: It's right by the county line. About 30 miles from downtown.

MARY: That's too far to walk.

SHIRLEY: Or wheel.

MARY: So, we have to figure out how to get from the delivery man's next stop to Holly's house.

BETTY: We could hitch a ride.

MARY: What about Shirley? How are we going to hitch a ride with her in that wheelchair?

BETTY: We're headed to the country, right? I'm sure we can flag down a pick-up truck. Then we'll just toss Shirley in the back of the pickup and tie her down with some rope.

MARY (reaching for her notebook again): Let me put rope on my list.

BETTY: I learned some good knots when I was on the army base, Shirley. I tie a mean Granny-knot.

SHIRLEY: A knot just for grannies? That's genius.

BETTY: Or I can clove-hitch or hog-tie you.

SHIRLEY: I don't care if you strap me in with barbed wire, just don't leave me behind.

MARY: Never. Right, Holly?

HOLLY: No man left behind. That's how they do it in the movies.

BETTY: So, we're a go?

HOLLY: We're a go. Betty, get to your lookout post.

BETTY (saluting): Roger.

HOLLY: Mary, assemble the supplies.

MARY: Right away.

HOLLY: Shirley, prepare yourself for decoy duty.

SHIRLEY: Will do.

HOLLY: All right, girls. This is it. Remember, "he who is brave is free."

BETTY: Who said that?

SHIRLEY: Holly did.

HOLLY: Let's move.

SCENE 4

NANCY is rummaging through the closet in her office looking for picnic supplies.

NANCY: I've got to have something in here to spruce up this picnic.

There is a knock at the door.

Who is it?

HOLLY: It's Holly.

NANCY: What do you want?

HOLLY: Can I come in?

NANCY: You know how busy I am.

HOLLY: This will only take a minute.

NANCY: Fine. Come in.

HOLLY enters.

Is there something you wanted?

HOLLY: I just wanted to stop by to see if you needed an extra hand in the kitchen. I figured you'd be spending most of your time down by the lake.

NANCY: I have to be all over the grounds today. I have a lot of things to manage.

HOLLY crosses to the window and looks outside.

HOLLY: It looks like they could use you outside right about now.

NANCY: Why?

HOLLY: I think they're having some trouble by the picnic tables.

NANCY: What?

HOLLY: Mr. Levi is dressing the salad.

NANCY: What's wrong with that?

HOLLY: He forgot to dress himself.

NANCY: It's like the Mother's Day tea all over again.

HOLLY: You better get down there.

NANCY: I don't have time for this today.

NANCY crosses to the window.

(Yelling out the window)

Mr. Levi, you're long past the stage where anybody wants to see that. Get back inside and put some pants on.

HOLLY: I don't know. Grace Louise Johnson is down there, and she seems pretty interested.

NANCY *(still yelling out the window)*: Grace Louise, keep your hands to yourself. If I have to come out there and separate you two, you're going to be on bread and water for a week.

HOLLY: You'd better go.

NANCY: Why are you so anxious to get rid of me? What are you up to?

HOLLY: Nothing.

NANCY: Look, Holly, I don't know what's going on, but I'm warning you, today is not a good day to mess with me.

HOLLY: Is there ever a good day for that?

NANCY: All I ask is for a little cooperation.

HOLLY: You don't want cooperation; you want obedience.

NANCY: I want you to follow the rules! Granted, this is a concept that is apparently foreign to you. You seem determined to buck the rules at every turn.

HOLLY: And that's saying something because there are a lot of rules to buck. Let's see. Lights out at 9 pm, no eating in the bedrooms, no late night fraternizing with the other cellmates. Oops, I mean residents.

NANCY: Those rules are for the health and welfare of all our guests.

HOLLY: What about the rule that confined Betty to her room for two days because you caught her with a cigarette?

NANCY: This is a nonsmoking facility.

HOLLY: Or when Mary wasn't allowed to eat dinner because you thought you smelled alcohol on her breath.

NANCY: We can't have inebriated residents.

HOLLY: Or when you withheld Shirley's medication because you said it made her unruly?

NANCY: That was for her own good. She needed time to settle down. She was getting out of control.

HOLLY: And that's what it's all about, right? Control. You want to control us.

NANCY: Of course, I want to control you. I'm in charge. I can't have the inmates running the asylum!

HOLLY: That's how you think of us? You think we're all insane? I've got news for you, lady, we're old, we're not nuts.

SHIRLEY wheels in carrying fireworks.

SHIRLEY: Check it out, Holly. Look what I found.

HOLLY: Not now, Shirley.

NANCY: What are you doing here?

SHIRLEY: Oh, it's you. I didn't think you'd still be here.

NANCY: In my own office?

SHIRLEY: I thought Holly would have gotten rid of you by now.

HOLLY: Shirley, keep still.

NANCY: Gotten rid of me?

SHIRLEY: Um, I mean...

HOLLY: Shirley just means she thought we'd be at the picnic by now, setting up.

SHIRLEY: Yeah, that's right.

NANCY: What have you got there?

SHIRLEY tries to hide the fireworks.

SHIRLEY: Nothing.

NANCY: Are those fireworks?

SHIRLEY: Yes.

NANCY: Where did you get them?

SHIRLEY: I found them.

NANCY: Where?

SHIRLEY: In the janitor's closet.

NANCY: And what were you doing in the janitor's closet?

SHIRLEY: I... uh...

HOLLY: I'm sure she was just helping Creepy Larry, I mean Larry, set up for the fireworks display tonight. Weren't you, Shirley?

SHIRLEY: Yeah, that's it.

NANCY: I don't know what you two are up to, but you need to hand over those fireworks right now.

HOLLY *(to Shirley):* You better give them to her.

SHIRLEY hands the fireworks to NANCY. Nancy takes them and crosses to the closet. Still holding the fireworks, she turns to HOLLY and Shirley.

NANCY: I'm going to lock these up so tight that you crazy old broads will never get them.

SHIRLEY: Crazy? Who are you calling crazy?

NANCY: If the shoe fits...

SHIRLEY: I don't like to be called crazy.

HOLLY: Calm down, Shirley.

NANCY: Yeah, Shirley, don't do anything crazy.

SHIRLEY: You want to see crazy?

SHIRLEY wheels toward NANCY. She grabs the fireworks from her and pushes her into the closet.

Holly slams the closet door shut and places the desk chair under the knob, locking Nancy in the closet.

NANCY: Hey! What are you doing?

SHIRLEY: Who's crazy now?

NANCY: You are, you crackpots.

HOLLY: Oh, my goodness, what have we done?

SHIRLEY: We've secured the prisoner!

NANCY: Open this door.

HOLLY: Should we open it?

SHIRLEY: Now who's crazy?

HOLLY: You're right. In for a penny, in for a pound.

NANCY: Let me out of here now.

HOLLY: I think you're getting a little unruly. You need some time to settle down.

NANCY: You're going to pay for this. When I get out of here, I'm going to make your lives a living torture.

HOLLY: Too late.

SHIRLEY: When you get out of there, we'll be long gone.

HOLLY: Yeah, and you and your rules can kiss my droopy, white keister!

HOLLY and SHIRLEY exit with the fireworks.

SCENE 5

MARY and BETTY are now dressed in all black with pantyhose over their heads. Mary is pacing nervously while Betty is looking toward the kitchen.

MARY: Everyone should be gathering by the front door for the picnic. Do you see the delivery man yet?

BETTY: I could get a better look if you'd let me take these ridiculous pantyhose off my head.

MARY: Keep those on. We don't want to be recognized.

BETTY: Then you shouldn't have used sheer pantyhose. You can see right through these things.

MARY: No, you can't. Plus, it's the only kind I had.

BETTY: Didn't you have anything in black?

MARY: Nice girls don't wear black stockings.

BETTY *(pulling the pantyhose off Mary's head)*: I don't think that rule applies if you're wearing them on your head!

MARY: Fine. I guess we'll blend in better without the stockings.

BETTY: Maybe if it were Halloween, but you don't see a lot of elderly women come to the Fourth of July picnic dressed like Catwoman.

MARY: Say what you want, but black is what everyone in the movies wears when escaping into the night.

BETTY: It's noon!

MARY: Well, it's also very slimming. You look really cute in that outfit, Betty.

BETTY: Good, since it's probably what they'll bury me in when we get caught.

MARY: Don't say that. You're courting bad luck.

BETTY: Oh, you and your superstitions.

MARY: I can't help it. Marvel Ann used to tell me that talking about your own death was the same as wishing for it.

BETTY: There are worse things than death.

SHIRLEY wheels in carrying the fireworks.

SHIRLEY: Wait til you hear what we did.

MARY: Shirley, there you are.

BETTY: Where have you been?

SHIRLEY: Never mind that. Guess what Holly and I did.

BETTY: What?

MARY: Where is Holly?

HOLLY enters.

HOLLY: I'm right here.

MARY: What's going on? What have you two been up to?

SHIRLEY: We've been taking out Nurse Nasty.

MARY: You didn't hurt her, did you?

HOLLY: All we did was lock her in her closet.

SHIRLEY: I almost gave us away, but Holly fixed everything.

HOLLY: Nevermind that now. Any sign of the delivery man?

BETTY: Not yet.

SHIRLEY: Good, because I still have to work on my distraction. I'll see you girls later.

MARY: Where are you going?

SHIRLEY: I need some more supplies. First stop: arts and crafts.

HOLLY: Don't go far. You have to hear when Betty signals that the delivery man has arrived.

SHIRLEY: Don't worry. You can count on me.

> *SHIRLEY exits.*

HOLLY: Okay, girls. Status report.

MARY: I'm doing well with supplies.

HOLLY: Good. What have you collected so far?

MARY *(going through a large bag)*: I've got some comfortable clothes for all of us. A first aid kit in case of emergencies and some . . .

> *A clear jar tumbles out, which MARY quickly returns to the bag.*

BETTY: What was that?

MARY: Nothing.

HOLLY: Come on, let us see it.

MARY: It was nothing. Just something I wanted to take with me.

BETTY *(grabbing the bag from Mary)*: Give it to me.

HOLLY: Stop, Betty.

BETTY *(getting the jar and looking at it)*: What is this?

MARY: It's just a tonic I need.

> *BETTY unscrews the lid of the jar and smells the contents.*

BETTY: Tonic, my Aunt Fanny. This is pure grain alcohol.

MARY: Give that back to me. It's the last jar I have from home.

HOLLY: What do you know?

BETTY: Little Miss Goody Two-Shoes is a bootlegger.

MARY: Don't be ridiculous.

BETTY: I never would have believed it. But I got to hand it to you, this family firewater of yours has given us the makings of a real party. I hope you packed some food in that sack or we're all going to be flat on our derrieres after chugging on this.

MARY: Of course, I packed food. See.

MARY pulls a large can of creamed corn from her bag.

BETTY: Creamed corn! You packed creamed corn!

MARY: It's all I could find.

BETTY: I'm not eating that stuff.

MARY: Fine, then you can just starve. It was hard enough for me to sneak this out of the kitchen. What did you want me to do? Drop in a rib roast and some fresh baked apple pie?

BETTY: As if you could find fresh apple pie in this joint. The closest we get to apple pie is Apple Brown Betty. I hate Apple Brown Betty.

MARY: Stop complaining. I don't have any Apple Brown Betty in here either.

BETTY: Good because I don't like it. I resent being served it every Sunday. Why does everyone think old people like Apple Brown Betty?

MARY: I have no idea, but it doesn't really matter because I don't have apple pie or Apple Brown Betty. All I have is creamed corn.

HOLLY: All right, enough. It's fine, Mary. Betty, when we get to my house, I'll bake you a fresh apple pie with apples right from the tree in my front yard.

MARY: You have an apple tree, Holly?

HOLLY: A huge one, with some of the sweetest apples you'll ever taste. We've always got a barrel of apples in the cellar. We'll sit on my front porch and eat apple pie. How does that sound?

MARY: Like a little slice of heaven.

BETTY: A little slice of apple pie heaven.

A truck pulls up. The motor keeps running.

MARY: What's that?

BETTY: It's got to be the delivery truck. Everyone else would have parked out front.

HOLLY: It looks like we're a go. All hands on deck. Mary, stow those supplies. Betty, sound the alarm.

BETTY lets loose with a whistle. MARY crosses to look for Shirley.

Mary, do you see Shirley?

MARY: No sign of her.

BETTY: Didn't she hear the whistle?

HOLLY: I can't believe this. This was all her idea, and now she's going to screw up everything.

MARY: What are we going to do?

BETTY: Girls, I hear him coming.

HOLLY: He expects to meet Nurse Nancy. We're going to have to explain why she's not here.

BETTY: Don't look at me. I'll only antagonize him. Let Mary handle him.

MARY: Me? Why me?

BETTY *(putting on a fake southern accent)*: Because you understand the fine art of conversation. You can charm him.

HOLLY: She's right, Mary. You're the best person for the job. We'll be close by if you need us.

> *HOLLY and BETTY hide. Mary grabs the jar of moonshine and takes a big swig. GUS enters carrying a large box in front of him. He can't see Mary.*

GUS: Hey, Nancy. Are you in here? Should I leave this stuff in the kitchen or do you want me to take it down to the picnic?

MARY *(flirtatiously and loudly)*: Well, hello there.

> *GUS drops the box.*

GUS: Lord, have mercy, you scared the bejesus out of me!

MARY: I'm so sorry.

GUS: It's all right. You just weren't who I was expecting.

MARY: I heard your truck pull up, and I wanted to come see your package.

GUS: What?

MARY *(pointing to the box)*: Your package. I thought it might be for me.

GUS: Oh, no, ma'am. It's just food for the picnic.

MARY *(holding out her hand in a formal manner for him to take)*: Oh, please, call me Mary. Let's not be formal.

GUS *(not sure what to do with the hand at first, then shakes it vigorously)*: Uh, nice to meet you.

MARY: And you are?

GUS: Gus.

MARY: Augustus, what a lovely name.

GUS: Uh, thanks.

> *GUS starts to pick up the box, getting ready to leave.*

I guess I'll just leave this in the kitchen.

MARY: Can I give you a hand?

GUS: No, no, that's okay.

MARY: Are you sure? After all, it's my fault you lost your load.

GUS: What?

MARY: If I hadn't startled you, you'd still have a hold of your package.

GUS: No, I wouldn't. I mean... It's not your fault. I should have brought some help.

MARY: Yes, handling that large a package does look like a two-person job. I'm up for it if you are.

GUS: No, really, it's okay. I can handle my own package. I mean I don't need any help!

MARY: Are you sure?

GUS: Yeah, I'm sure. I'm just going to unload these picnic supplies and be on my way.

MARY: Did you bring wieners?

GUS: Excuse me?

MARY: Wieners? Did you bring wieners? It's not Fourth of July without them in my book.

GUS: Oh, sure, I brought... wieners.

MARY: What about buns? I like nice, soft buns.

GUS: Yeah, I have buns, too. Everything's in here.

GUS points to the box.

MARY: Well, let me help you get inside this box.

GUS: No, really, I'm just going to leave it here and be on my way. I left my motor running and I'm low on gas.

MARY: No, you can't go.

GUS: Why not?

MARY: Because we're not ready yet.

GUS: Ready for what?

MARY: Uh, nothing.

GUS: What are you up to, lady?

MARY: Why, Gus, whatever do you mean?

GUS: You've been acting cuckoo ever since I came in here.

MARY: Cuckoo?

GUS: Yeah. Are you funny in the head or something?

MARY: Well, I never! Just because I'm on the other side of 60 doesn't mean I've lost my senses.

GUS: Then you're up to something.

MARY *(calling to Holly and Betty)*: He's on to us, girls.

BETTY and HOLLY emerge.

GUS: Hey, what's the idea? How long have you two been hiding there? I'm going to get Nancy.

HOLLY: Now, Gus, let's not do anything rash. There's no need to involve Nancy.

GUS: I say there is. You three seem mighty suspicious to me.

HOLLY: Gus, you have the wrong idea. We're just looking for a ride into town. We have a few errands to run.

GUS: You want me to give you a ride into town?

BETTY: That's right.

GUS: You must think I'm stupid or something. I know you're not allowed to leave this place.

MARY: It's just for a little day trip. We'll be coming back tonight.

GUS: And how are you planning on getting back? Am I supposed to hang out while you run your errands and then drive you back here like I'm some kind of chauffeur?

MARY: Oh, Gus, that would be so sweet. Would you do that?

GUS: Heck, no, I won't do that.

HOLLY: You can just drop us off downtown and go on your way. We'll get back here somehow.

BETTY: Yeah, we can always hitchhike.

GUS: Who's going to pick up bunch of old lady hitchhikers? A wacko, that's who. I'm not taking you ladies into town and leaving you there.

HOLLY: Gus, really, we don't have time to argue about this.

BETTY: We need you to give us a ride.

MARY: We're running out of time.

HOLLY: Now march through that door and take us to your truck or else.

GUS *(laughing)*: Are you threatening me? What are you going to do? Beat me to death with your canes? Stab me with your knitting needles? Poison me with milk of magnesia? I know you outnumber me, but believe me I'm not too worried. I think I can take you.

> *BETTY hits GUS with a can of creamed corn from MARY's supply bag. She knocks Gus out cold. Truck engine stops running. Stunned silence.*

HOLLY: Crap.

Blackout. End of Act I

ACT II

SCENE 1

MARY *(whispering)*: Oh, my, heavens. Betty, what have you done?

BETTY: He had it coming.

HOLLY *(crossing to Gus to feel for a pulse)*: He's not dead, but he's out cold. What did you hit him with?

> *BETTY holds up the can of creamed corn.*

Creamed corn?

BETTY: I guess this stuff has a use after all.

MARY: You didn't have to knock him up.

BETTY: Out! I knocked him out! Do you ever listen to yourself?

MARY: What are you talking about?

BETTY: You've been talking dirty for the past 10 minutes and you didn't even realize it.

MARY: You told me to flirt. That's all I was doing.

BETTY: Women usually charge for flirting like that.

MARY: Well, I never.

BETTY: I bet you have.

HOLLY: Nevermind. It doesn't matter now. We've got bigger problems. We've got to subdue Gus in case he comes to. Did you remember to pack rope in that bag?

MARY *(retrieving rope from her supply bag)*: Here you go, Holly.

HOLLY: Don't just stand there you two. Help me tie him up.

> *As the WOMEN are tying up GUS, SHIRLEY enters draped in red, white, and blue crepe paper and wearing a Statue of Liberty headpiece.*

SHIRLEY: What are you doing?

MARY: Shirley!

HOLLY: Where have you been?

BETTY: And why do you look like you've been run over by a parade float?

SHIRLEY: They're making these headpieces in the arts and craft room. Everyone's going to wear them to the picnic today and then we're going to parade around the lake.

HOLLY: Haven't you forgotten something?

SHIRLEY: What?

HOLLY: We're not going to the picnic!

SHIRLEY: Why not? I love picnics.

HOLLY: You were supposed to be creating a distraction for us. We're trying to get out of here today.

SHIRLEY: I'm sorry, Holly. I guess I got distracted myself.

HOLLY: Sorry doesn't cut it, Shirley. Because of your absentmindedness, Mary's had to practically prostitute herself, Betty might get charged with aggravated assault, and we're all about to commit grand theft auto.

SHIRLEY: All that happened while I was in arts and crafts?

HOLLY: Things are moving fast, Shirley, and apparently you can't keep up. We're going to have to leave you behind.

MARY: Holly, no.

BETTY: Don't say that.

SHIRLEY *(looking stricken)*: You would leave me behind?

MARY: Of course, not.

BETTY: Holly didn't mean that.

SHIRLEY: You think I'm a feeble-minded old biddy in a wheelchair, don't you? Admit it.

BETTY: Let's face it. We're all feeble-minded old biddies. Only feeble-minded old biddies could come up with a scheme like this. And yes, you're in a wheelchair, but that just means you can move faster than the rest of us.

MARY: That's right. Those wheels are an asset not a liability.

BETTY: If the screws give chase, who's going to get away first? My money's on you and those four wheels.

SHIRLEY: That's kind of you, but I know I'm a liability. I wasn't always this way, you know. I've only had to use this chair for the past couple of years, just since my hip gave out. I know it's selfish of me to want to come with you, but I can't help it.

HOLLY: You're not the one who's being selfish, Shirley, I am. It's just that I've got to get home today.

SHIRLEY: I know. It's your last chance.

MARY: We'll get you home, Holly.

SHIRLEY: If we put our feeble-minds together, we'll figure out a way.

BETTY: That's easier said than done. In case you haven't noticed, our plan has kind of derailed.

BETTY points to GUS.

SHIRLEY: What happened?

BETTY: He met with the business end of a can of creamed corn.

MARY: How are we getting into town now?

HOLLY: We'll have to drive ourselves.

MARY: Anyone still have an active driver's license?

BETTY: That's what you're worried about? We'll be driving a stolen vehicle but as long as we're licensed everything will be fine.

MARY: Not stolen, borrowed. We're bringing it back tonight.

HOLLY: Okay, listen up. I'm going out to start the truck. You girls find somewhere to stash Gus. Then grab the supplies and meet me outside.

HOLLY exits. BETTY, MARY, and SHIRLEY stare at GUS.

BETTY: What are we supposed to do with him?

MARY: Let's see if we can drag him under the table.

MARY and BETTY try to drag GUS.

BETTY: Nothing but dead weight.

MARY: Don't say that. It's bad luck.

SHIRLEY: Here, girls, let me help you.

BETTY: What do you plan to do? Roll over him and ground him into more manageable chunks?

SHIRLEY: Grab some of that rope. We'll tie it to Gus and my chair. Then you two can push us to the table and we'll stash Gus under it.

BETTY: Piece of cake.

BETTY and MARY tie a rope between GUS and SHIRLEY. They try to push the wheelchair to the table but can't manage it. They give up and instead pick up the table and place it over Gus. They untie the rope around Shirley and collapse on the sofa.

SHIRLEY: That went well. What's next?

Outside HOLLY tries to start the truck. The engine revs and then dies. The THREE WOMEN look at each other in panic. Holly enters.

HOLLY: It won't start. It's out of gas. I can't believe this is happening.

BETTY: What kind of delivery man makes his rounds on an empty gas tank?

SHIRLEY: I guess he was in a hurry.

BETTY: That's no excuse.

MARY: Now to be fair, he didn't know we'd be borrowing his truck today. I'm sure if he did, he would have filled it up.

SHIRLEY: What are we supposed to do now?

MARY: I guess it's just not meant to be.

BETTY: What do you mean by that?

MARY: Maybe we're not meant to leave here.

HOLLY: You put that idea right out of your head. I'm getting out of here today.

MARY: But, Holly, how are you going to manage that?

HOLLY (exploding): I don't know!

> *HOLLY grabs the Statue of Liberty headpiece.*

Maybe I'll wear Shirley's headpiece and ride out in the parade.

> *HOLLY grabs the pantyhose Mary and Betty wore earlier and puts them on her head, pulling them over her face.*

Maybe I'll disguise myself and hijack Mr. Munsen's scooter.

> *HOLLY pulls the pantyhose off her head and wraps them around MARY's neck.*

Maybe I'll take a hostage and demand a ride into town.

BETTY (pulling Holly off Mary): Holly, calm down. We'll figure something out.

HOLLY: I'm sorry, girls.

MARY: It's probably all for the best.

BETTY: Of course, you'd say that. You never wanted to break out in the first place.

MARY: I never said that.

HOLLY: She's got a point, Mary. You've been trying to back out all day. Do you even want to leave?

MARY: Yeah, sure.

BETTY: You don't sound very sure.

MARY: It's just that I'm...

HOLLY: What?

MARY: I'm scared.

BETTY: Of what? Nancy and Gus?

MARY: It's not just them. I'm scared to leave Happy Meadows.

BETTY: For the love of God, why?

MARY: Because it's my home! It's the only one I have.

BETTY: We're coming back tonight.

MARY: But what if something goes wrong? What if we can't get back or they won't let us come back?

SHIRLEY: Then we'll be together. That's all the home we need.

MARY: You girls are like a family to me.

SHIRLEY: Even Betty?

BETTY: Hey.

MARY (smiling): Betty most of all.

BETTY: And here I am biting your head off.

MARY: Just like family. All right. I can do this as long as we're in it together. So, what's the plan?

HOLLY: We need some time to get that truck working.

SHIRLEY: I'll get you some time, Holly.

HOLLY: What?

SHIRLEY: You wanted me to create a distraction, right?

HOLLY: That was the original plan.

SHIRLEY: And that's what I'm going to do.

HOLLY: I don't know, Shirley.

SHIRLEY: Please, Holly. Let me make it up to you all.

HOLLY: What are you going to do?

SHIRLEY: You'll see. I just need a few minutes to get something I left in the arts and crafts room. Then I'll create a distraction you'll never forget.

HOLLY: All right. Meet us at the truck as soon as you're done.

SHIRLEY exits.

MARY: Now what do you think that was all about?

HOLLY: With Shirley, who knows?

MARY: I'm not sure we should have let her leave here alone.

BETTY: Yeah, she's not exactly batting a thousand today.

HOLLY: That's for sure. She almost gave away our plan to Nurse Nancy. She wasn't here to distract Gus. And it's only a matter of time before Nancy escapes and comes after us.

BETTY: That's quite a day's work.

HOLLY: If we get caught, it's going to be on her head.

MARY: Now we can't blame everything on Shirley. We're all in this together.

BETTY: We're all going to be in the hoosegow together if she keeps up with this stuff.

MARY: Don't say that, it's bad luck.

HOLLY: I just hope she doesn't make things worse.

BETTY: I don't know how things could get any worse. We're stuck.

MARY: I have faith in Shirley. She'll come up with something.

BETTY: That's what I'm afraid of.

HOLLY: It's going to have to be something miraculous or else our goose is cooked.

SHIRLEY yells, "Give me liberty or give me death." Sound of fireworks exploding.

MARY: Holy Hannah! What was that?

BETTY: One guess.

HOLLY: That didn't sound good.

> HOLLY and BETTY race to the door to see what is happening.
> MARY cowers behind.

MARY: I can't look. Tell me what's happening. Is it Shirley?

HOLLY: I'm not sure. It's hard to tell.

BETTY: Is that her?

HOLLY: Where?

BETTY (pointing): Over there.

MARY: What's she doing?

HOLLY: I think she's fleeing the scene of the crime.

MARY: What crime?

HOLLY: Betty, look down the hall at the arts and crafts room. There's smoke pouring out of it. Shirley must have set off those firecrackers.

MARY (hopping up and pacing frantically): Oh, dear. Is Shirley okay?

HOLLY: It hasn't slowed her down any. She's wheeling full speed down the hallway heading for the front door.

> Smoke starts to fill the common room. GUS crawls out from
> under the table, pulls off the rope, rubs his head, and exits
> unseen by the women.

BETTY: The smoke is getting really bad. I can't see very well. Where are my glasses? Is that her?

HOLLY: No, that's Mr. Levi.

MARY: Does he have his pants on?

HOLLY: No, but there's Grace Louise Johnson, and she has his pants on.

BETTY: Is that Shirley? What's she carrying?

HOLLY: She's got a bunch of star-shaped balloons in one hand and she's waving an American flag with the other hand. It looks like...

MARY: What?

HOLLY: Oh, no. It can't be.

MARY: Just say it.

HOLLY: I think she's on fire.

MARY (running around in panic): Oh, no. I'll sound the fire alarm. Somebody get the extinguisher. We've got to put her out.

> BETTY runs and grabs the fire extinguisher. MARY runs to the
> alarm on the wall and pulls it. Nothing happens.

MARY (CONT'D): Dad-burn-it. The alarm is broken. Doesn't anything work in this place?

BETTY *(as if she's storming the beach at Normandy)*: I've got the extinguisher. Let's go.

> *SHIRLEY wheels through the common room with sparklers attached to her wheelchair. NANCY and GUS follow.*

SHIRLEY: How's this for a distraction, girls?

NANCY: Get her, Gus.

GUS: I'm trying, but she's a speedy little devil and my head is killing me.

> *SHIRLEY, NANCY, and GUS exit. Sounds of fireworks subside. Smoke begins to dissipate.*

HOLLY: That's our cue. We're not going to get a better distraction than this. Get to the truck.

MARY: But it's still out of gas.

HOLLY: Any ideas, Betty? You're the mechanic.

> *BETTY looks around the room and then grabs the jar of moonshine.*

Really, Betty, we're on the clock. This is no time for a drink.

BETTY: I don't plan on drinking it.

HOLLY: What are you doing with it?

BETTY: Gas substitute.

MARY: What?

BETTY: I figure if this stuff can get Mary's engine racing, it might rev up that broken down delivery truck. It's worth a shot. Let's go.

MARY: But what about Shirley?

HOLLY: We'll have to hope she gets away and makes it to the truck.

> *Sound of a loud crash.*

SHIRLEY *(offstage)*: Help, girls, help. They've got me. The screws have got me.

MARY: Oh, no. They've captured Shirley.

BETTY: We've got to help her.

> *BETTY and MARY start to exit. HOLLY stays behind.*

MARY: Come on, Holly.

HOLLY: But this is our chance to escape. We're not going to get a better one.

MARY: But Shirley needs us.

HOLLY: I'm sorry, girls. I've got to get to Jimmy. He's family.

MARY: We understand.

BETTY: You got to do, what you got to do.

>*BETTY tosses HOLLY the jar of moonshine.*

Pour it in the tank, turn her over, and pray.

MARY: Be careful, Holly.

>*HOLLY crosses to leave.*

SHIRLEY *(offstage)*: Somebody, help!

>*MARY and BETTY exit. Holly turns back to the empty room.*

HOLLY: Good luck.

>*HOLLY exits.*

SCENE 2

NANCY's office.

NANCY: All right, Shirley, what's the skinny?

GUS: Yeah. Why did those old harpies hit me over the head and tie me up?

NANCY: And what's the big idea of setting off those fireworks?

GUS: And where's the rest of your gang?

NANCY: Well?

GUS: Spill it, lady.

SHIRLEY *(looking confused)*: Where am I?

NANCY: You know darn well where you are.

GUS: Happy Meadows Nursing Home.

SHIRLEY: What's going on?

GUS: I'll tell you what's going on. *(To Nancy)* What's going on?

NANCY: It's a ploy.

SHIRLEY: Who are you and why are you yelling at me?

GUS: Oh, man. I think she's gone 'round the bend.

NANCY: Don't be ridiculous. She's faking it.

GUS *(shaking his finger at Shirley)*: Are you faking it, lady? Because if you're faking it, that's not very nice.

SHIRLEY: Faking what? And stop shaking your finger at me. I don't know what you two want from me. I just stopped in to pick up some bagels and lox, but I can't seem to find the deli counter.

GUS: I don't think she's faking it.

NANCY: She always did have a short leash on reality.

GUS: I think the leash has snapped.

NANCY: Shirley, this isn't a grocery store. This is where you live.

SHIRLEY: Don't be ridiculous. Why would I live in a grocery store?

NANCY: It's not a grocery store! It's Happy Meadows Nursing Home.

SHIRLEY: Well, it certainly doesn't look very happy around here. And neither one of you looks very happy either.

NANCY: I'm not happy. I've spent the past 30 minutes locked in a closet only to escape in time to find that you've knocked out and tied up my delivery man and practically burned down my nursing home.

SHIRLEY: I see. What about you? What bee is in your bonnet?

GUS: There's no bee in my bonnet. I just don't like being knocked unconscious by canned goods.

SHIRLEY: Then you should be more careful when you're stocking the grocery store shelves.

NANCY: This isn't a grocery store!

SHIRLEY: He's a stock boy, isn't he?

GUS: I'm a delivery man. I brought the food for your picnic. I didn't expect to be seduced, bludgeoned, and tied up by a gang of old ladies. I wasn't even supposed to work today. It's a holiday, you know. I'm heading back to my truck and going home.

SHIRLEY: You can't.

GUS: Why not?

NANCY (suspiciously): Yes, why not, Shirley?

SHIRLEY (looking nervous): No reason.

> SHIRLEY starts to hum "When Johnny Comes Marching Home."

GUS: Forget it. She's crazy.

NANCY: Oh, she's crazy all right, crazy like a fox. Did you really think I'd fall for this poor, demented fool routine?

GUS: What's going on?

NANCY: What was the plan, Shirley? Were you supposed to distract us? Get us out of the way? What are your pals up to?

SHIRLEY: I won't talk. You can't make me.

GUS: What's happening?

NANCY: It's a ploy. She's been trying to keep us occupied. She doesn't want us to know what her friends are up to.

GUS: What are they up to?

NANCY: I have no idea, but I'm sure gonna find out.

> NANCY grabs SHIRLEY's wheelchair and starts to shake it.

You better start talking, Shirley.

SHIRLEY: Stop, you're making me sick.

> GUS stops NANCY from shaking SHIRLEY.

GUS: Whoa. Settle down. There's no need to get violent.

NANCY: We need to find out what these old ladies are up to by any means necessary.

GUS: I don't think so, Nancy.

NANCY: What do you mean?

GUS: It was one thing to skim some profits, but I'm not going to hurt anybody.

SHIRLEY: You've been skimming profits? Is that why this place is falling apart and the food is so bad?

NANCY: That is none of your business.

SHIRLEY: It sure is my business. I'm the one who has been living on prunes and bisque. And you were in on this, Gus?

GUS: I—

NANCY: Don't answer her.

GUS: But I—

SHIRLEY: How could you do this? I'm ashamed of you, young man.

GUS: I didn't mean any harm.

SHIRLEY: It's all fun and games until somebody gets hurt.

GUS: I guess I just didn't think.

SHIRLEY: That's no excuse.

GUS: I know, I'm—

SHIRLEY: What would your mother say?

GUS: That does it. Sorry, Nancy. I can't do this anymore.

NANCY: It's not that easy, Gus. You're in too deep, and I have no intention of letting you bring me down.

GUS: I'm not going to squeal on you. I just want out.

NANCY: You really want to go back to being just a wage slave? No more perks?

GUS: I lived without the money before, I can do it again.

NANCY (*seductively*): But what about me, Gussy? Can you live without me?

GUS: Well, we could still get together.

NANCY: I don't think so, Gus. I need a man who's there for me.

GUS: But I don't want anyone to get hurt.

NANCY: The only one who's going to get hurt, Gus, is your wife, when I tell her everything you've been up to.

SHIRLEY: You're married?

GUS: Technically.

SHIRLEY: Shame on both of you.

NANCY: Spare us the lectures. What's it going to be, Gus? Are you sticking with me or do I rat you out to the wifey?

GUS: All right, you got me. I don't know why I ever got involved with you in the first place. Just lonely, I guess.

NANCY: Or horny. Now come on. We've got to capture those old ladies before the inspector gets here.

SHIRLEY: Inspector? What inspector?

NANCY: The state inspector is on his way to make sure everything is up to code around here.

SHIRLEY: Boy, is he in for surprise.

NANCY: There won't be any more surprises today. Not once I catch your partners.

SHIRLEY: You'll never catch them.

NANCY: I caught you, didn't I? Come on, Gus. We'll leave her here and lock the door from the outside.

SHIRLEY: Oh, please, don't lock me in. I don't like being locked in.

NANCY: Well, I don't like being shoved in closets, and Gus here doesn't like to be tied up. *(Pause)* You don't do you?

GUS: No!

NANCY: Your friends didn't think about what we like, so why should we think about what you like? Come on, Gus. We've got to find them.

GUS: I'm sorry, Shirley.

> *NANCY and GUS exit. SHIRLEY starts to rock back and forth.*

SHIRLEY: I don't know if I can take this. I can't stand being locked up in here. *(Wheeling herself to the door and banging on it)* Hey, somebody, get me out of here. *(Banging some more and then giving up)* It's no use. *(Wheeling back to the desk and picking up the phone)* Maybe I could call for help. *(Staring at the phone and then hanging it up)* Who could I call? *(Spying the intercom)* Maybe I can get a message out through this thing. *(Pushing buttons on the intercom)* Attention, attention. Old lady being held against her will in the main office. Send reinforcements. I will not be imprisoned. Remember Pearl Harbor. Remember the Alamo. Remember the Maine.

> *SHIRLEY starts to sing "Halls of Montezuma." BETTY appears at the window.*

BETTY: For God's sake, Shirley, put a sock in it.

SHIRLEY: Betty! You found me.

BETTY: It would have been hard not to.

SHIRLEY: What are you doing here?

BETTY: We're here to bust you out.

> *BETTY starts to climb through the window.*

SHIRLEY: We? Is Holly with you?

> *MARY appears behind BETTY, who is halfway in and halfway out the window.*

MARY: No, Shirley. It's Mary.

SHIRLEY: Oh, Mary. I'm so glad you're here.

MARY: Of course, I'm here. I wouldn't have left you for anything, Shirley. I said to Betty...

BETTY: Hold on there, Chatty Cathy. Do you mind if we table this chit-chat until my tush is no longer hanging out an open window?

MARY: Oh, I'm sorry, Betty.

BETTY: Give me a shove so I can get through.

> *MARY gives BETTY a push and Betty crawls inside.*

SHIRLEY: Oh, Betty. I'm so glad to see you.

> *SHIRLEY tries to hug BETTY.*

BETTY: Settle down. We've got no time for that.

> *MARY leans in the window.*

MARY: Oh, Shirley. I'm so glad you're all right. We were worried sick about you. I told Betty we had to find you and as soon as I said that we heard you over the intercom. We were going to come in the door, but we saw Nancy and Gus lock it. That's when we decided to come through the window. I knew you'd be working yourself into a...

BETTY *(interrupting)*: Is this really where you want to have this conversation, Mary? Get inside before someone arrests you for breaking and entering.

MARY: Give me a hand, girls.

> *BETTY and SHIRLEY pull MARY through the window.*

SHIRLEY: I'm so happy you came to save me, but where's Holly?

BETTY: She's gone.

SHIRLEY *(starting to cry)*: Oh, my, God. Was it her heart?

MARY: No, sugar. She's not dead.

BETTY: She just left.

MARY: You know how important it was for her to get home today.

SHIRLEY: Thank, goodness. It's best she left. I was only holding her back. Just like I'm holding you two back.

MARY: Don't say that.

SHIRLEY: I appreciate your coming, but it's no use. I can't get out through the window in my wheelchair. You two have to leave without me. If you hurry, maybe you can still catch Holly.

BETTY: Nothing doing. We're in this together. We'll figure something out.

SHIRLEY: We don't have time. Nurse Nasty and Gus are looking for you.

MARY: No man left behind, Shirley, remember?

SHIRLEY: I know, but things have gotten out of hand. You can't waste any more time on me.

BETTY: Either we all get out or none of us do.

> *HOLLY appears at the window.*

HOLLY: That's right. One for all and all for one.

BETTY, SHIRLEY & MARY: Holly!

The WOMEN rush to help HOLLY climb through the window.

MARY: What are you doing here?

BETTY: We thought you left.

HOLLY: I couldn't leave.

MARY: But you may have lost your only chance to escape.

SHIRLEY: What about Jimmy?

HOLLY: Jimmy's family but so are all of you. And family sticks together.

MARY: Oh, Holly, we're so glad you came back.

BETTY: Yeah, we need you. Because I can't for the life of me figure out how we're going to get Shirley out of here.

SHIRLEY: Listen to me, all of you. I'm grateful you came back for me. You're the first people in here who've treated me like an equal. Everybody else always kept their distance from Crazy Shirley. But you girls came back for me, like I mattered.

MARY: Of course, you matter.

SHIRLEY: I know that now, and I'll remember it for the rest of my life, but you've got to get out of here before Gus and Nancy come back. Just go back the way you came.

HOLLY: That's exactly what we're going to do. And you're coming with us.

SHIRLEY: I can't climb through that window like the three of you.

HOLLY: You can't climb but maybe you can slide.

SHIRLEY: Slide?

HOLLY: We could back you up to the window, tip the wheelchair, and slide you out.

MARY: She'd land on her head!

BETTY: Would that really matter?

MARY: She could be seriously injured.

HOLLY: We're on the ground floor and the bushes will break her fall.

MARY: I don't think it's worth the risk.

HOLLY: What do you think, Shirley? Is it worth the risk?

SHIRLEY: You're darn-tooting. Let's do it.

HOLLY: Atta girl. Okay, Betty, you're the strongest. You're going to have to help me tip her out the window.

BETTY: Whatever you say, Sarge.

MARY: I'm not sure this is our best idea.

HOLLY: Do you have any other ideas?

MARY: Not really.

HOLLY: Then help us back Shirley up to the window.

MARY: I don't like this.

SHIRLEY: Man up, Mary. I'm the one getting tossed out the window.

MARY: Oh, all right. I'll help.

> *HOLLY, BETTY, and MARY wheel SHIRLEY so that her back is facing the window.*

BETTY: Let's do this.

MARY: Be careful of her bad hip.

HOLLY: Are you ready, Shirley?

SHIRLEY: United we stand. Divided we fall.

MARY: It's the fall I'm worried about.

HOLLY: Okay, on the count of three. One. Two.

> *The WOMEN start to tilt the wheelchair so that SHIRLEY will slide out the window backwards. NANCY and GUS enter.*

GUS: What the...

NANCY: Stop!

SHIRLEY: Don't stop, girls. Let her rip.

> *SHIRLEY tries to fling herself out of the window but the women put the wheelchair back on the floor.*

HOLLY: It's no use.

MARY: We're caught.

BETTY: Like rats in a trap.

NANCY: Just what do you lunatics think you're doing?

SHIRLEY: We're making a break for it, so don't try to stop us.

> *SHIRLEY tries to climb out of the window, but GUS stops her.*

GUS: Be careful, Shirley. You might get hurt.

NANCY: Don't go soft on me now, Gus. We've got major damage control to do.

GUS: What do you mean?

NANCY: We've got to get rid of these troublemakers before Inspector Monroe gets here.

GUS: I told you I'm not cottoning to any violence.

MARY: What are you going to do to us?

SHIRLEY: Bring it on, Nursie. Do your worst.

BETTY: Shut up, Shirley. Aren't we in enough trouble?

MARY: You wouldn't let her hurt us, would you, Gus?

SHIRLEY: Don't count on Gus to do the right thing. He's a slave to the weakness of the flesh.

MARY: Aren't we all?

GUS: I'm sorry, Shirley. I'm sorry all of you. You deserve better than this.

NANCY: I'm the one who deserves better. Something better than this thankless job and middle-aged boy toy.

GUS: You know what, Nancy. I think I'm the one who deserves better.

BETTY: You tell her, Gus.

GUS: Better than a blackmailing battle-ax of a girlfriend who's clueless when it comes to treating a real man right.

MARY: Oh, my.

GUS: I deserve a chance to be free of all this.

SHIRLEY: Sing it, sister.

GUS: I deserve the chance to say, "Hey, world, I may be a middle-aged delivery man with a low income and a bad marriage, but my name is Gus and I deserve better."

> *MARY, HOLLY, BETTY, and SHIRLEY cheer.*

So, Gus is claiming his independence, and things are going to change around here.

NANCY: What do you plan on doing?

GUS: Here's what.

> *GUS grabs NANCY.*

NANCY: Are you out of your mind?

MARY: Gus, what are you doing?

> *GUS shoves NANCY in the closet and shuts the door.*

GUS: Don't just stand there gawking. Help me.

> *HOLLY hands GUS the chair.*

HOLLY: Put this under the knob.

NANCY: You're going to pay for this.

GUS: I'm done paying.

NANCY: Let me out.

> *NANCY starts to bang on the door.*

GUS: Look, you ladies had better get out of here. I don't know how long I can hold her.

MARY: Oh, Gus. You're so gallant.

GUS: Don't make a whole big thing out of it. The way I see it is that I owe you. Now get going.

> *NANCY continues to bang on the closet door. GUS crosses to the office door to open it while SHIRLEY crosses to the window.*

SHIRLEY: We're free! Follow me, girls. Now, on the count of three, give me a good push out this window.

MARY: Shirley, honey.

SHIRLEY: Hurry up. We don't have much time.

HOLLY: Shirley.

SHIRLEY: Come on, move it.

> *BETTY whistles loudly.*

BETTY: Why don't we try the door this time?

> *SHIRLEY notices them all standing at the door.*

SHIRLEY: Oh, yeah, good plan.

GUS: Get the lead out, ladies.

NANCY: What's going on out there? Gus, you better not be letting them go.

GUS: That's exactly what I'm doing.

> *SHIRLEY starts to wheel to the door.*

SHIRLEY: Free at last! Free at last!

> *SHIRLEY exits humming "God Bless America."*

BETTY: Thanks for the help, Gus. And sorry I creamed you with the corn.

GUS: No problem.

> *BETTY exits joining in the humming of "God Bless America."*

NANCY: Gus, you're going to be sorry for this.

GUS: Not as sorry as you're going to be.

MARY: Oh, Gus. You're so brave. If only I could think of some way to show my appreciation.

HOLLY: Don't start that again. Just thank him and scram.

MARY: Thank you, Gus.

> *MARY kisses GUS on the cheek and exits. NANCY bangs harder on the closet door.*

HOLLY: Are you sure you know what you're doing?

GUS: Don't worry about me. You take care of those ladies.

HOLLY: Will do. And we'll bring your truck back soon.

GUS: I hope by the time you get back, I'll have things settled here.

HOLLY *(nodding toward the closet)*: Are you sure you can handle her?

GUS: After watching everything you ladies accomplished today, I feel like I can handle anything.

HOLLY: Thanks, Gus. You've truly made this an independence day.

> *HOLLY exits. GUS crosses to the closet door and pounds on it.*

GUS: Settle down in there. I've got business to attend to.

> *GUS crosses to the desk and starts to look through Nancy's papers.*

NANCY: What are you doing out there?

GUS: I'm looking for a phone number.

NANCY: Who are you calling?

GUS *(dialing the phone)*: The inspector. I want to know what's keeping him.

NANCY: Gus, think about what you're doing.

GUS *(into the phone)*: Hello? I'm calling from Happy Meadows Nursing Home.

NANCY: Gus, if I go down, you go down.

GUS: Is this Inspector Monroe? Are you on your way?

NANCY: Gus, stop.

GUS: Yes, there's definitely a problem. I'll fill you in on everything when you get here.

NANCY: Noooooooooo.

> *Blackout.*

SCENE 3

Lights up on the WOMEN seated together eating apple pie as the sun sets.

SHIRLEY: I can't take it anymore, I tell you. I just can't take it.

MARY: What could possibly be wrong now, Shirley?

SHIRLEY: I can't eat another bite. I just can't.

BETTY: Then pass your piece my way. This is the best apple pie I've ever tasted.

SHIRLEY: The perfect ending to the perfect day.

MARY: Where's Jimmy, Holly?

HOLLY: Look out there. See him down by the barn? He can't wait for the fireworks to start.

SHIRLEY: Neither can I.

BETTY: I would have thought you'd had enough fireworks for one day.

SHIRLEY: I'm keeping a safe distance this time.

BETTY: Good girl.

MARY: I love fireworks. They're so romantic. I wonder what Gus is doing now? I hope he's not in too much trouble.

HOLLY: He said he was going to turn Nancy in. I bet they go easy on him.

MARY: I hope so. I'd hate to think of him locked up all alone on Independence Day.

BETTY: If they lock him up, we'll bust him out. We're getting good at it.

MARY: All we need is some rope.

SHIRLEY: Some fireworks.

BETTY: And a can of creamed corn.

HOLLY: All the ingredients for an Independence Day we'll never forget.

The WOMEN start to hum "When Johnny Comes Marching Home." Sound of fireworks. Lights fade.

END OF PLAY

ABOUT STAGE RIGHTS

Based in Los Angeles and founded in 2000, Stage Rights is one of the foremost independent theatrical publishers in the United States, providing stage performance rights for a wide range of plays and musicals to theater companies, schools, and other producing organizations across the country and internationally. As a licensing agent, Stage Rights is committed to providing each producer the tools they need for financial and artistic success. Stage Rights is dedicated to the future of live theatre, offering special programs that champion new theatrical works.

To view all of our current plays and musicals, visit:

www.stagerights.com

Made in United States
Orlando, FL
14 March 2023

31035873R00028